Contents

Chapter One – Know The Combination

Chapter Two – Challenge Your Ability

Chapter Three – Having A Vision

Chapter Four – Role Models

Chapter Five – The Winning Edge

Chapter Six – Change Your Thinking

Chapter One

Know The Combination

As a coach, teacher and mentor I have been afforded many opportunities over the past twenty years to examine the secrets of success. I saw a man do a demonstration using a combination lock to illustrate the differences between successful and unsuccessful people. He pulled two people out the audience and handed the first individual a lock along with the combination. He asked the first individual to open the lock using the combination he was given. The first individual turned the lock three times to the right, then two times to the left and one time to the right and successfully open the lock. He called the second individual, giving him the very same lock minus the combination and asked him to open it. He looked confused at first and then started turning the lock to the right, then to the left and back to the right. After a few minutes of attempting to open the lock he gave up.

The point is you can't be successful at anything you attempt if you don't know the combination to the thing you are attempting. You may know two of the numbers in the combination, but if you want to successfully open the lock you must have all three numbers in the combination. It doesn't matter if you are black or white; male or female the lock is going to open if you know the combination. We have to stop making excuses and start figuring out the combination to being successful. Do you read enough about the subject matter you want to succeed in? How much time are you putting in each day in preparation for success?

5 P's Of Success

When I was in junior high school, my teacher gave the class a handout that had the 5 P's of Success on it. We had to learn what they were and be able to communicate it in our own words. The 5 P"s are:

Proper
Preparation
Prevents
Poor
Performance

The 5 P's of Success taught me that if you properly prepare yourself in whatever you are doing, you will prevent yourself from having a poor performance. If you have a test and you have properly prepared yourself by studying, it is almost impossible to fail. However, if you don't go about studying the proper way you are going to fail. Many people will invest large amounts of time doing things incorrectly only to fail. Those people are failing because they are not doing things the proper way. It has been stated that "practice makes perfect" but I believe that statement is not totally accurate. It should be stated that proper and perfect practice makes perfect. It does not profit you to practice doing a thing the wrong way. All you are doing is developing bad habits. It takes a long time to stop doing something that has become routine. As the saying goes "Bad habits are hard to break." Webster defines habit as " The tendency or disposition to act in a certain way, acquired by repetition of such acts." Habits are things in life that we do so often that it comes as second nature. These are the things we do without having to think about it. Habits, when done correctly, can be beneficial or work against you when done incorrectly.

If I worked on making a left hand lay up because it was my weak hand and I would continue to work long and hard doing it incorrectly. Then I would have wasted a lot of time working on something doing it the wrong way. This is why understanding the "5 P's of Success" is important. In everything you do it must be done in the proper way or you will have develop a bad habit.

It wasn't until later in my adult life that the 5 P's of Success really began to make sense to me. I have been applying these principles for over twenty years. In all my years of coaching, I had all my players learn these principles and understand what it really means to apply them. They could not enter the gym to practice if they couldn't explain to me the 5 P's of

Success. As I entered the gym for practice, all the players were shooting around and getting loose. The start of practice would be signified by the blowing of my whistle and the gathering of players at center court. I told the guys that they all needed to go to the foyer area of the gym and I would call them back individually. They were told in the hallway that they could not enter the gym for practice unless they could explain in their own words what the "5 P's of Success" meant. As I entered the hallway to call in the first player I notice that they seem to be nervous about this task. To my surprise the majority of them gave great answers. I'm proud to say after over twenty years, my former players can still quote it and explain what it means. There is a young man who played for me that is now coaching AAU basketball and he's using those same principles with his team.

Doing More

I was reading the book called "The Prayer of Jabez" and it stated that you have to be gimpers in order to be successful. At the time , I had no idea what being a gimper meant. The author stated that a gimper was someone who does more than what's required or expected of them. As a former college basketball player I applied that principle to my life and as a coach, I taught that principle to my players. The player or athlete who spends two hours extra working on his game is the one that's going to be successful. I emphasize extra because you need to do more than everyone else. If you only do what everyone is doing how do you distinguish yourself from others. Bill Bradley played professional basketball for the New York Knicks and is now a Senator in New York. Bill used the gimper attitude to become a successful NBA basketball player. After each practice he would stay and shoot extra shots. He would not leave the gym until he makes 15 shots in a row from 5 difference spots on the court. If he missed on the 14th shot he would have to start all over again. Now that's doing more than what's required or expected. Bill has won two NBA Championships.

I heard a professor talk about the big difference between 211 and 212 degrees. I was amazed by the differences that one degree can make. Although both are very hot, 212 degrees is at a boiling point while 211 degrees is just really hot. When something is boiling it produces steam and steam has the power to move a locomotive. Two hundred and eleven degrees can not move that locomotive. My point is if you go that extra degree or just one more mile you can be successful.

We must know that becoming successful comes with a price. Nothing in life worth having is free.
When things get a little tough you have to be willing to take the pain that comes with success. T.D. Jakes said that "the struggles of my past are the fertilization to my future." Therefore, everything you go

through in life should be a great opportunity for your growth. The struggles in life are there to make you stronger. Take a butterfly for instance, before it becomes this great insect and flies gracefully through the air it has to go through some tough times. It starts out in the form of a caterpillar inside a cocoon. The only way a butterfly can be released from the cocoon is to use its weak wings and make them strong by breaking through the cocoon. If someone would have freed that butterfly from the cocoon before it's wings were strong enough it wouldn't have been able to fly. We have to strengthen ourselves before we can take on certain responsibilities. "When things go wrong as they sometimes will, and when the road you are trudging seems all up hill, rest if you must but don't you quit".

In order for us to know the combination to success we must be willing to educate ourselves and study to be the best at what we do. So many times we are passed over for jobs or promotions because we didn't know the combination. We may have had two of the numbers correct to the combination but the third number is crucial if we're going to open the lock. In life you are going to get opportunities and when they come you must be ready for them. There's a quote that says "It's better to be prepared for and opportunity and not have one, then to have one and not be prepared". I recall a situation that presented itself to a friend of mine that is a great example of this. He had wanted to be a high school basketball coach. He was coaching a junior varsity team and was very successful. After the season ended, the varsity coach decided he no longer wanted to coach. The opportunity for my friend to have the job presented itself but he wasn't ready. He was not a candidate for the position because he didn't meet all the requirements for the job. He knew what he needed to do, but kept procrastinating. This is a classic example of not being prepared when the opportunity comes. Great opportunities only come around so often, that's why it's vitally important that you are prepared to unlock the door to your success.

Grateful

Each day of our life, we need to develop an attitude of gratitude. How many times during the day do you speak negative things out of your mouth? I'm confident that most people throughout the course of the day spend more time thinking negative thoughts opposed to positive thoughts. Our lives always line up with our thoughts and with that being said it is of the utmost importance that everyone speak positive and be grateful for each day.

Recently I started writing down the things that I'm grateful for and speak them aloud each day. On my list of things that I'm grateful for is my health and strength and my family. I'm grateful for my wife and children, our home, our transportation and my job just to name a few. I could list many more but you get the picture. When you are grateful for the things you have in life, you always find more things to be grateful about.

I saw a quote the other day about gratitude and it stated "gratitude is like a muscle, the more we do with it the stronger it gets." So I challenge you today to begin to identify all the things big and small that you are grateful for even the small things.

The other day I worked a twelve hour shift at my job, and I was tired and wanted something good to eat. My wife and I don't always agree on the same food choices. She text me on my way home and stated she had cooked and I didn't have to stop and get anything. I was relieved that I didn't have to stop and excited to see what she had prepared for me. The meal she prepared was not my favorite nor did I eat it very often. After working a twelve hour shift and on my feet most of that time, I was not very grateful for that meal. After a few minutes of being upset, it dawn on me that I should be grateful for that meal even if it wasn't my favorite, because you have third world countries that would love to have food of any kind. So many times we take the little things for granted instead of being grateful. My wife asked me how was the meal and I have to admit it was pretty good because I change my attitude to be grateful for all things. I'm also grateful I have a wife who would take the time to cook for me.

There was another situation that happened to me that made me upset and ungrateful. In the span of about eight weeks I had one of the worst times of my life financially. I lost a few thousand dollars in a bad deal. My car needed repairing and that cost a few hundred dollars. Then another car needed a motor and a few days later another car was in an accident. While all of this was happening our daughter was preparing to move out of town and needed her car for her new job. So we are now carpooling and doing whatever it takes to get to our destination. At this time I'm starting to feel a high level of frustration. I have been doing things the correct way and treating others the way they should be treated and all these things start happening to me and my family. I've been working overtime at my job so my wife and I could enjoy some vacation and travel. However it seemed the more overtime I worked, more issues requiring money kept coming up. It seemed we were paying out for other things and not our vacation plans. As I was sharing this with my wife, she stated that just because you are doing things the correct way doesn't mean that things aren't going to happen to you. We have to look at every situation as positive.

Once I got myself together I realized that we were able to do everything we needed to do and go every place we needed to go. I began to understand that sometimes in life you are going to be thrown a curve ball that tries to take you off your focus. I have learn that it's not what happens to you that matter, it's how you respond to it. When you respond with the right attitude things always workout. My family and I try to focus on all the good things that has happened in our lives because it is the most difficult thing to do in a trying time. After embracing gratefulness, it changed everything. I realize that I should have been grateful for what I had and not worry about what I didn't have.

Persistence

I recalled a story I was told several years ago that spoke of a man who wanted to go to college and play football. He was not the biggest or fastest guy in high school, but displayed a great work ethic to go along with his positive attitude. He came from a family of migrant workers who moved around following the crops from Georgia to Florida. It was a difficult time for migrant children to get an education because they were only allowed to attend school in the morning. At noon they had to go to work in the fields until sunset.

Now living in Florida and completing high school, this young man wanted to attend Bethune-Cookman College in hopes of playing football. After arriving at the school he noticed that there were over 100 students trying out for the 40 available spots on the team. On the final day of tryouts he was called to the coaches office and told he didn't make the team.

His high school coach told him of another school that he could possibly try out for in North Carolina. The college coach was a friend of this high school coach. He packed up his things and headed to North Carolina. After arriving in North Carolina and meeting with the coach, he was told there were no open spots on the team and he needed to return back home to Florida. He was willing to do anything to make the team.

Some of the players heard about what happened and suggested he spend the night on a sofa in the lounge of the football dorm. The next morning he saw the other players preparing for practice and wondered what he could do to be noticed by the coaches. He notice that the players left the locker room in a mess. So he began to clean the locker room while they were practicing and cleaned it again after practice was over. He had to do something because going back home was not an option. He was determine to enroll in school and play football.

The head coach was made aware of the things he had been doing in the locker room and for the team. The coach told him that he would give him a meal ticket for the rest of the week and a place to sleep. The coach also told him to get with the trainer and give him a hand. He insisted that he would have to leave by the end of the week.

It was Friday and the assistant coach told him that

the head coach wanted to see him. After hearing this he knew the coach was about to ask him to gather his things because his time here was up. But the coach had something else he wanted to discuss with him. He was told that one of his players was hurt and he had and opening on the team if he still wanted it. He was overwhelm that he was finally getting the opportunity to play.

After having a great college career on the field and in the classroom, he graduated with his law degree and moved back to Florida and started his law practice. Today he is a very successful lawyer and has donated 10 million dollars to the school that gave him a chance.

This great man whom I'm referring to is Attorney Willie Gary. The greatest message here is that you must be persistent, and never give in, never give up and never give out. It could have been so easy for him to have gone back home, but he knew that he was close to opening the lock to success. So many times in life people often choose the easy way out. They don't stay on course and do whatever it takes to become whatever they want. This is why in the "pyramid" of life it's crowded at the bottom, and very few at the top. There is so much room at the top but we will not do the things that it will take to get there. The only people that make it are the people in life that refuse to take "no" for an answer like Willie

Gary. They will look for other ways and options to navigate on the road to success.

Chapter Two

Challenge Your Ability

During my senior year of high school, I was being recruited by several colleges to play basketball. It was stated to me by school officials that I would never graduate from college. At the time I was a little perplex by that statement, because I felt like I could and would graduate from any college I chose to attend. At the time I wasn't exactly knocking the ball out the park with my grades, but they weren't all that bad either. According to the effort of my grades I might understand why they stated I would never graduate from college. Besides I was just another jock who only focus on basketball and not academics.

That statement, I will never graduate from college was the best thing that could have happen to me at the time. I'm the type of person who if you told me I couldn't accomplish something I was going to prove you wrong. So when I decided to attend Jacksonville University in the Fall of 1980, I had made up my mind that I was going to graduate even if it took me more than four years. I received my B.S. Degree in Education in 1984 (4years). This was one of the greatest accomplishments of my life, because people doubted that I could do it. My point behind telling you this story is that this situation could have made me bitter or better. I chose the latter. When someone tells you that you can't do something, that should set something off in you that motivates you to prove them wrong.

Never Put A limit On Yourself

You should never put a limit on what you can do and never let anybody tell you what you can't do. Philippians 4:13 states "I can do all things through Christ which strengthens me." Too many times in life most people wait for someone to challenge them. The quickest way to failure is waiting for others to get you going. There are two types of people who are never successful: Those who wait to be told what to do; those who do only what they are told to do.

When my three children were growing up, I would allow them to do things and go places based on their maturity level. What I mean by that is, if I have to keep telling you the things you should already be doing such as keeping your room clean, taking out the trash or washing the dishes then you can't be trusted. If you can do those things without having to be reminded each day, then my wife and I would be willing to give them more freedom.

But if you chose not to do those things that needed to be done, then we would tighten up the rope and you had less freedom. When you do things without being told you loosen the rope to more freedom.

Don't Quit

I was given a poem by my coach titled "Don't Quit" I fell in love with that poem the minute I read it. Each stanza had so much power that after reading it you felt like you would never give up or quit on anything you attempt. I love the poem so much that I made my basketball team learn at least one stanza of it. And as you would guess I would not allow them to enter the gym if they couldn't quote one stanza.

Don't You Quit

When things go wrong as they sometimes will,
When the road you're trudging seems all up hill,
When the funds are low and the debts are high,
And you want to smile, but you have to sigh,
When care is pressing you down a bit
Rest if you must, but don't you quit

Life is queer with it's twist and turns,
As everyone of us sometimes learn,
And many a fellow turns about
When he might have won had he stuck it out
Don't give up though the pace seems slow
You might succeed with another blow

Often the goal is nearer than
It seems to a faint and faltering man
Often the struggler has given up
When he might have captured the victor's cup

And he learn too late when the night came down
How close he was to the golden crown

Success is failure turned inside out
The silver tint in the clouds of doubt
And you never can tell how close you are
It might be near when it seems afar
So stick to the fight when you're hardest hit
It's when things seem worst that you must not quit
                                    Author Unknown

Keep Trying

The greatest mistake you can make is to be afraid of making one. People who don't make mistakes in life are people who never try. The most successful people in the world made many mistakes before they got it right. Henry Ford had five businesses that failed and left him broke before he founded the successful Ford Motor Company. Bill Gates dropped out of college and failed in his first business attempt with Microsoft co-founder Paul Allen called Traf-O-Data. While this early idea didn't work, his later work did, creating the global empire that is Microsoft. Harland David Sanders better known as the Colonel of Kentucky Fried Chicken, was rejected 1009 times before a restaurant accepted it. Thomas Edison in his early years was told by teachers he was too stupid to learn anything. He was fired from his first two jobs for not being productive enough. He made 1000 unsuccessful attempts at inventing the light bulb before getting it right. These are just a few successful people in the world who didn't get it right on the first go round. The lesson in this is that they never quit or gave up.

Never To Young or Old

In my research and study on success, I found that a number of individuals have become successful in their older years. No matter how old you are now, you are never too young or too old for success or going after what you want. Here's a list of people who accomplished great things at different ages.

- Helen Keller at the age of 19 months, became deaf and blind. But that didn't stop her. She was the first deaf and blind person to earn a Bachelor of Arts Degree.
- Mozart was already competent on keyboard and violin: He composed from the age of 5
- Shirley Temple was 6 when she became a movie star on "Bright Eyes".
- Anne Frank was 12 when she wrote the Diary of Anne Frank
- Magnus Carlsen became chess Grandmaster at the age of 13
- Jessie Owens was 22 when he won 4 gold medals in Berlin 1936
- Roger Bannister was 25 when he broke the 4 minute mile record

- Oprah was 32 when she started her talk show, which became the highest rate program of it's kind
- Martin L. King Jr. was 34 when he wrote the speech " I Have A Dream"
- Abraham Lincoln was 52 when he became President
- Ronald Reagan was 69 when he became President
- Nelson Mandela was 76 when he became President of South Africa

After a successful freshman basketball season in high school, my wife and I decided to transfer our son to another school within the same county. When we registered him for school the following year, we were notified by the coach that our son would not be eligible to participate in sports that year but was allowed to attend the school.

We were told that someone from my son previous school reported to the High School League that we are transferring our child because of basketball. Because of these allegations he would not be eligible. Basketball was one of the reasons we transferred our son but not the main reason for making that decision. We live about 25 miles from the previous school our son was attending and the one we transferred him to was only 11 miles. Our son would be driving to school and we didn't want him to have to make that round trip drive of about 50 miles as a beginning driver. We felt that the other school would be better for him all around and not just for sports. I graduated from that high school and wanted to see my children graduate from there as well.

After being denied we had to come up with another option for him to be eligible to play basketball that school year. After talking to school officials we were told of our option and they were not good ones. We were told that we would have to get a house in the city of the school being transferred to. We at the time lived in a different county then the other two schools. Because my wife is an employee in that county we are allowed to send our children to those schools. We would also have to put our house up for sale as well. So things aren't looking to good at this point. This means we would have to take on two mortgages just for him to play basketball that year. I don't know many who can take on that type of responsibility or be willing to try. So we as a family came together to pray about what direction we should pursue. After a few days in prayer we decided to try and make the move happen.

Shortly after, we were able to find a place to move and put our house on the market. I'm still looking back at this situation and we are amazed how God worked everything out. Our son went on to play that year and had probably his best high school season that year. Two years later he won a state championship and was invited to play in the North-South All-Star game for seniors. He was named the most valuable player of the all-star game. He received a four year basketball scholarship and has graduated from college and is gainfully employed. Never give up and don't quit.

When I was ten years old my father died of a heart attack and left my mother with six children. I had three older sibling who at the time could take care of themselves. That left me and my two sisters with one being my twin. My mom worked at Oxford Sewing Plant for $3.35 an hour or $4.00 an hour if she made production. Trying to support a young family on that salary was tough and trying at times. My mom was only 32 years old at the time of my fathers death. She was young and could have thrown in the towel and given up, but she never gave up or gave in. She was dedicated to supporting her family. Along with her job at Oxford she also work from home with her clothing business. She is one of the best seamstress around and she had more than enough work to support her family. I don't remember a time when we didn't have everything we needed. We might not had all the things we wanted but our every need was met. The majority of the clothes we wore were made by my mom. And I must say we were always dressed nice. I'm grateful to my mother for never giving up on her family and being a positive role model in my life. She didn't say a lot but lead us by example.

> Never Give In
> Never Give Up
> Never Give Out

The Hurdle

When my daughter entered her freshman year of high school, she was preparing to tryout for the basketball team. During her workouts after school, she met another freshman who was also preparing to tryout for the team. They became friends and after about ten years they are still friends and both have completed college.

During those ten years a lot has happen with my daughter's friend. At the age of sixteen she found out that her mother had cancer. At this point she was thriving on the playing field and in the classroom. After the death of her mom, I had the opportunity to talk with her about her feelings and surviving without her mother during the pivotal years of growing into a young lady. I asked her how she was able to stay focus and continue her education during such a difficult time. She stated it was very hard and honestly wasn't focus on anything. Her mom died a month before her high school graduation and that really put a damper on things and graduation was the last thing on her mind. Her desire to graduate wasn't there anymore because her mom would not be among the crowd to witness it and she definitely didn't care about college at this point.

Her next hurdle was to survive without her support system. She stated that she had no idea where she was going to live and who would support her because her mother was the only person that she ever depended on. She had many relatives offering advice about what she needed to do and where she should live. She decided to follow her own path and listen to her heart to determine what she was going to do next. So she decided to accept an offer from her friend of ten years to stay with her and her family. She stated that was one of the best decisions that she made.

After going through all of this, she was able to regain her focus and get her life back on track. The beauty of this story is that she went on to graduate from high school with honors. After graduation she attend college on a track and field scholarship. In 2014, she graduated from college where she was on the Dean's List all four years and is now working on her masters while working a full-time job.

So many times you hear about situations like hers and they don't always come out successful. This young lady worked very hard to accomplish what she did. She did the majority of it on her own. This is a great example of, "It doesn't matter what happens to you in life, it's how you choose to handle what happens to you." She was face with an incredible hurdle and overcame it.

Chapter Three

Having A Vision

One Sunday morning several years ago, I attended a church whose sermon topic was " Where there is no vision, the people perish". I'd heard that scripture in Proverbs quoted on many occasions, but for some reason it spoke to me in a different way. In my life, I began to understand that if you don't have a vision you would end up on the other side of success.

In the early 90's, I was teaching at an elementary school in Florida. I was approached by a parent who was willing to pay me to teach her son the basic fundamentals of the game of basketball. I agreed to work with her son twice a week to improve his basketball skills. After a few weeks of training this student, I was approached by more parents who were interested my services. I was working with three students per week and being compensated for my efforts. As the summer approached, I envisioned having a summer camp that would allow any child who wanted to learn about basketball to attend. That summer we had about 15 students attend the camp. This was the beginning of "Vision Basketball Camp".

In 1995, I moved back to my home town and started Vision Basketball Camp at one of the local middle schools. Since that time we have had hundreds of campers who have attended the camp. The neat thing about this camp is that some of the campers who attended when they were younger are now participating as counselors. The camp is growing each year and has been a big part of the community during the summer. This camp has been featured on two of the local television stations and special guests have included professionals basketball players and coaches. If I had not heard the sermon about having a vision this camp probably would have never started.

As I have had the opportunity to work with the youth in the community for the last twenty plus years, I noticed that so many of our youth were falling behind in school and as a result, dropping out. I noticed that gang activity, in my community, was on the rise and our youth with no vision were gravitating towards the gangs. The prison systems are over crowded and more prisons are being built just to accommodate our young people.

Deeply disturbed by the problems our youths are facing, I envisioned myself as apart of the solution and not apart of the problem. I believe it is easier to teach them now opposed to having to rehabilitate them in the long run. Matthew 9:37 states that "the harvest is plenteous but the laborers are few". If we don't give back to these youths in our communities we will lose them to the prison system, gangs and death. Young people are our future and they need to be well equipped to handle it. We have to teach them to, "Have character and not be a character." When I was teaching, if a teacher needed to step outside the classroom for a minute, they would instruct the class to stay seated and no talking. As soon as the teacher steps outside the noise and moving around the classroom begins. This is a sign of not having character. Many people are aware of the problems with our youth and discuss it each day, but many are not willing to take action. We preach about these things on Sunday morning and that's where it stops. Talk is cheap and we have got to be about putting our money where our mouth is. This is not a knock on any one person, this is a call to get everyone to begin to make a difference in the lives of today's youth.

In July of 2013, I met with one of my former players and we decided to start a program to help with the growing problems concerning our youths that was mention earlier. We started the youth program, "Vision Academy" and named it that because of the sermon I heard. The vision sermon resonated deep in my spirit and spurn me into action.

Vision Academy is designed to teach our youth the fundamentals of life and basketball. We meet with a group of young men once a week for a two hour session. The first hour is spent in the classroom discussing life skills and character building exercises. The second hour of our program is focus on teaching the fundamentals of basketball. We believe that knowledge of these fundamentals are essential to their success. We have several community partners, one in particular, teaches a 16 week session on Healthy Relationships. At the end of the 16 week session, they are tested to see what they have learned. After which another topic is explored.

We are grateful for our partners in the community. We have various leaders from the community and surrounding areas to come and speak to our youths. We are currently serving over twenty students at this time. We meet with the parents of these youth at least once per month to keep them abreast of what we are doing and what we need them to be doing as well to assist us in helping their child be successful.

As I drive through my city, I see individuals who had potential for a promising future but somehow lost their vision. We all know that life has a way of throwing curve balls. We must learn that the situations we encounter on the journey to our destination is only temporary. Most of us give up instead of pressing on or starting over. I believe that there are several components that an individual must posses in order to be successful. The purpose of Vision Academy is to equip young men with everything they need to be a success.

We must begin to set goals. Goals in our lives should serve the the same function as a GPS does in our car, they should help navigate us through life. It's not just enough to say you have goals, you must write them down and put them in a place that you can see each day. I recently started a vision board for my life. A vision board highlights all the things you want to accomplish in life and aids in keeping you motivated and focused. You find pictures of those things you want and put them on your board. After completing the board, you should place it where it can be viewed daily. Seeing what you want to accomplish should motivate and keep you focused on your goal. A constant reminder should prompt you to do something each day to help you reach your goals. If you don't have it where you can see it you are going to miss days without doing anything. Another thing I do with my goals is to put them on 5x7 index cards and keep them in my pocket. I can pull them out and look at them any time and ask myself what have I done today to help me reach my goals.

Visualization

A high school coach took three basketball players with similar free throw shooting abilities and demonstrated the power of visualization. The first player could not practice or shoot free throws for 30 days. The second player was allowed to practice free throw shooting for one hour each day for 30 days. The third player could not touch or practice shooting free throws, he could only visualize shooting them for 30 days. At the end of the 30 days, player number one who wasn't allowed to practice, improved 0%. Player number two, who practiced for an hour each day for 30 days, improved 24%. Player number three , who could not touch or shoot but only visualize shooting free throws, improved 23%. It's amazing how the player that was allowed to practice was only 1% better then the player who visualized himself making free throws. There is something to be said about the importance of not only practicing but visualizing the things you want to accomplish in life. Visualizing your goals as completed, the mind begins to line up, adjust itself and create the results.

86,400 Seconds

There are 86,400 seconds in a day. That's a lot of time we have to be productive or not productive. If you waste your seconds away on non-productive things, you have just thrown away a day that you will never get back or see again. A lot of times we feel that we can make up the time we lost on yesterday, but time lost is time lost and there's no way that you could ever make it up.

I read a book "One -on-One" by Coach John Wooden that stated, each day of our lives we are given 86,400 seconds. It's like God depositing that much money into your account each day. But you would have to spend the entire amount each day or you would loose it. That's a lot of money to loose because you didn't use it. It's the same way with our time, if we don't maximize the use of our time we lose it and we can never get it back. So I say to each of you reading this book, time is precious and it is all we have in life. We must make the most of each day.

I have stressed the importance of having goals, but I feel it's worth sharing it again. The major reason people waste large quantities of time is because they fail to set goals or establish a plan to help them navigate through the day. Without a plan, you waste countless time and energy going nowhere.

I recall when I was in college, I spent the better part of my time sleeping. If I was not in class or practice, you could find me in my room sleeping. As I became older I realized I wasted valuable time that could have been used to prepare for my future. While I was wasting time sleeping, others were planning and working on their future. They were working part-time jobs and honing there skills. They saved money in preparation for life after graduation. At this juncture in my life, I don't spend a lot of time sleeping. There's so much more I want to experience and do while I have the opportunity. If you ever get the opportunity to speak with someone who is successful, ask them what their daily routine is consist of. I'm confident that they aren't wasting the 86,400 seconds on non-productive activities.

I was listening to motivational speaker Willie Jolley speak and he quoted this poem that I love and share it often with the young people in our program.

It only takes a minute
60 seconds in it
Force upon me
Can't refuse it
Didn't seek it, Didn't choose it
But it's up to me to use it
I must suffer if I misuse it
Give an account if I abuse it
Only a tiny minute
But eternity is in it

Willie Jolley

Chapter Four

Role Models

A role model is a person whose behavior in a particular role is imitated by others. Someone who another person admires and tries to immolate. You can learn a lot from people that are around you each day. We can look at their experiences, to help guide us on our journey.

I believe everyone should have a role model. In our society today most of the role models are sports figures. There are many individuals unrelated to athletics that are great role models. Young people choose role models based on the outward appearance of wealth such as, cars, homes, and even stylish dress. We all know these are expendable things but a role model is someone who is striving to be the best and maintains integrity. I submit to you that when choosing a role model you should know just as much about that person's morals and values as well as their talent or skill. A role model should be someone who motivates you to become the best person you can be. They should be individuals who are doing or have done what you are striving to do.

My first role model was my high school basketball coach, who I met in 1978. I had the pleasure of playing my last two years of high school basketball for him. Until his arrival as coach, I never had colleges recruiting me or my teammates. He was the first to introduce me to summer basketball camp. With his assistance, I attended a college basketball camp and it proved very beneficial. The following week when I returned home, I began to receive numerous letters from colleges who were interested in me. After the letters started pouring in, coach made sure I was taking classes that would allow me to attend college. He helped all his players who expressed an interest in attending college and playing on the next level. My coach had an open door policy, anytime you needed him, he made himself available. He made us wear suit and ties to all of our away games. I wasn't excited about his dress code policy but in retrospect it really was a good thing. I learned that when you look good ,you feel good, and when you feel good you play good. Had this coach not come into my life I would not have attended college. He took the time to not only be a basketball coach but a life coach. He helped us in whatever capacity we needed him. I have tried to be available to my players and impact their lives in the same capacity.

In 1995, my wife and I along with our two children at the time were living in Florida, I received a call from my high school coach who was now the principal at one of the local middle schools. He told me that he had a counseling position open at his school and he wanted me for the position. I was surprised and excited to hear about the position as well as being offered the position. At the time my wife and I had no intentions of returning to my hometown. Everything was going well in Florida. After getting more information about the position, I told coach I needed to think about it and discuss it with my wife. After discussing it with my wife and praying about it, I contacted coach and told him I would take the position. I was excited about the opportunity to work with the man who had such a great impact in my life. The only reason my family and I are back in my hometown is because of my role model and high school coach.

The final person I want to share with you as one of my role models, is my college roommate. Before we ended up at the same college, we attended the same college basketball camp I spoke of earlier. Later that year we played against each other in the North vs South High School All-Star game. The thing that impressed me about him was his determination. During our freshman year in college, he was diagnosed with a degenerative hip disease that ended this college basketball career . He was dealt a hand that many individuals would not be able to handle. He spent the better part of his life working to play college basketball and now it was taken away. I was impressed with the way he handled the situation. He didn't hang his head which would have been understandable. He didn't quit school or stop being around the basketball program. He was able to keep his scholarship and still be a part of the team in other ways. He didn't let his situation make him bitter, it made him better. I can't say that I would have reacted the way he did. He went on to graduate at the top of his class and holds a high level position in the banking field. He has been bless with a great family and all are doing well. I'm grateful I had the opportunity to be around him during that time because I saw first hand how to take a negative situation and turn it into a positive one.

Who Are You Hanging With

It's very important to understand that you become much like the individuals who you choose as associates. If you hang out with drug dealers chances are you will become a drug dealer. If you hang around people who don't go to class, chances are you will not go to class. If you are spending time with individuals who make poor grades, you are probably going to make poor grades. On the other hand if you hang with positive people, you will become positive. You have to choose your associations carefully. You have to ask yourself the question, "What positive influences are they having on you, and what negative influences are they having on you?" Whether you know it or not, you are being influenced one way or the other. It's either positive or negative. The choice is yours.

The bible states that iron sharpens iron. In other words, the people that you choose to hang around and associate with are, the people you will ultimately become. People that you associate with strongly affect and influence you. When I was in school as a student and then as a teacher, I noticed that the students that made the best grades usually hung out together and the ones who made poor grades usually hung out together. I heard someone say "If you are the smartest one in your group, then you need to find a new group of people to hang around. I understand that others may be learning from you, but who are you learning from?

Don't let others dictate what you become or what vocation you choose. When you have opportunities for greatness, don't let your so called friends hold you back from those opportunities. I've learned that if they don't have the opportunity that you have, they may try to get you to remain at the bottom with them. We have to stop being envious of others and begin to celebrate their successes. If they can be successful it gives hope to others that they can be successful and reach goals, too.

If you are going to be successful in life you have to take control of your life. You are responsible for the places you go in life. We can't always take everyone with us who might want to go. A lot of people only want to hang with you to keep tabs on you and what you are doing, so they can keep you from reaching your dream and goals. These people are like vampires, they hang around to suck the life out of you. When my son was in college he told me about how his coach wanted them to be a team that worked together and not as individuals. So he talked to them about not allowing vampires on the team. These types of individuals will suck the life out of the team and they were not allowed to get on the bus if they didn't have the right attitude. They came together as a team and won the conference championship and received a bid to the NCAA tournament. It is very important to find and spend time with individuals that support you and who are making great choices in their lives. The people who don't increase you will inevitably decrease you.

Chaper Five

The Winning Edge

Winston Churchill stated that "Victory comes only to those who work long and hard and are willing to pay the price in blood ,sweat and tears." He also stated that "Hard work is the basic building block of every kind of achievement."

In preparation for my first year of college basketball in Florida, I decided to work hard to get in good shape. I wanted be ready when preseason conditioning started. Everyday I would left weights, run and play five on five until the street lights came on at night. After all the training from the summer I was ready to hit the college campus and impress the coaching staff and players with my conditioning. After being given a preseason workout schedule I was surprised at how much they did in their conditioning program. We had to run about 2 miles to the fitness center to lift weights and after doing so, run back. This was done at noon in "The Sunshine State", some of you may know what the August weather was like in Florida. Later that evening, we had to work on our game in the gym and play five on five. We did this each day leading up to the beginning of the season. Here I was thinking I was in good shape only to realize that I haven't even come close to the conditioning that was necessary.

Over the next four years, I was able to have a great college career, because I learned the importance of hard work in everything I did. There were days when I didn't feel like going to class because I was so tired from the workout the day before. Going to class according to my coaches was not an option. I began to understand that this was serious stuff. My entire body was aching for days. At this point in my brief college career, I was ready to throw in the towel. The next day I called home and talked to my family about leaving school, because it was more than I wanted to do at the time. But they convinced me to stick it out. By the time the season started, I was in the best shape of my life. This goes back to what Winston Churchill stated about paying the price in blood, sweat and tears. Believe me there was a lot of sweat and hard work to get into great shape.

As I think back on those days, I'm grateful for learning the importance of hard work. It's the reason I'm a college graduate today. Nothing in life is more gratifying than seeing your hard work pay off, be it in the classroom or on the playing field.

When my oldest son was in high school, he wanted to get a basketball scholarship to attend college. I told him he would have to work really hard and do the things that others weren't doing. We decided that he would workout before going to school to better his chances of earning the scholarship he wanted. His attitude was that he's going to be working and preparing his game while others were sleeping. He did this for about two years and from his hard work, he earned a scholarship as was mentioned in the earlier chapter. Getting up at 4:00am was not easy for a teenager let alone his father. I was the one passing him the ball and rebounding.

As a coach, one of the things that really got under my skin was players not working hard or giving the effort in practice. When this happens I would fuss and let them know about it. I had a special drill that we did when this would happen. It's called, " The Chinese Fire Drill." In this drill we would have half the players line up on one end of the court at the right side of the free throw line. The other half lined up on the other half of the court at the right side on the free throw line. Each group had a ball, and when I blew the whistle the person with the ball would run and throw the ball onto the backboard and the next person would have to catch it and throw it back up. Then they would run to the other end of the court and do the same thing. Both groups are now running full court and throwing the ball off the back board. The object of the drill was to not let the ball touch the floor. We usually have them do this drill for about three to four minutes. If the ball touches the floor before time expired they would have to start the drill over from the beginning. It only took a few minutes of that drill to get their attention and work harder. It doesn't matter if you have talent or not, if you put in the work you will come out on top. I read a quote that stated, " If you pay the price it's yours." If you go into the store and see something you like and you purchase it, the item becomes yours. It's the same in anything you want to accomplish. If you are willing to pay the price in hard work it's yours. It's just that simple. I read another quote that stated, "Hard work beats talent when talent refuses to work hard." This quote sums it all up. You don't have to be talented to be successful, you only have to put in the time and effort.

As a student-athlete, I had to understand that everything in college was based on being on time. We were expected to be in class on time each day. If we weren't on time there would be consequences. As a player we had to show up to practice and others functions on time. We were punished if we were late. The punishment would be a 6:00am study hall or an early morning run and I wanted no part of that. If memory serves me correct I was never late.
If practice was suppose to start at 3:00 and you showed up at 2:45 you were considered late. The expectation was, you should be dressed, have your ankles taped and on the court working on your game before the real practice started. If you showed up at 6:55 for a game that started at 7:00, you were considered late by basketball terms. The reason you are late is because you have to get dressed, taped, go over the scouting report, warm up and that takes more than five minutes. No matter what you are attending you should always give yourself some

wiggle room in case something occurs. In our family I'm a stickler for being on time and that's usually getting there 20 to 30 minutes before it starts. I'm the only one in my family that feels that way. It's hard to get them ready on time. Some believe that if it starts at 6:00 we should be leaving the house at 6:00. We are still working on this.

Positive Thinking

When I was coaching in the early 90's, my team was down by one point with three seconds left in the game. We had the ball and they fouled us and we were awarded two free throws. So I called time out to discuss what we were going to do. I gave instructions on what to do after Ty makes the free throws. We would put light pressure on them without fouling. Since Ty was not one of our starters I wanted to be as positive with him as I could. That's why I made the statement after he makes the free throws. Just as I expected Ty made both free throws and we won the game by one point. The next day I saw Ty's father and he thanked me for the positive encouragement I gave his son.

I remember hearing a story about a young lady who was stricken with cancer. After being told about her situation and the options available to her. She decided not to do chemotherapy and focus on her faith and being positive. She and her husband decided to watch comedy on T.V. to filled her time with laughter and being positive. Over the next few months all she did was laugh while she kept her faith. Within months she was cured of the cancer without any medication. Her positive thinking and laughing healed her of cancer. It's amazing the things that can happen if we have a positive attitude.

I came across a poem that talks about your thinking. It really hit home what I'm trying to articulate in this chapter. I want to share it with you.

If you think you are beaten, you are
If you think you dare not, you don't
If you'd like to win, but think you can't
It's almost a cinch you won't
If you think you'll lose, you've lost
For out in the world we find
Success being with a fellow's will
It's all in the state of mind
If you think you're outclassed, you are
You've got to think high to rise
You've got to be sure of yourself before
You can ever win a prize
Life's battles don't always go
To the stronger or faster man
But soon or later, the man who wins
Is the one who thinks he can

Walter D. Wintle

Get In Shape

I know you are wondering what being in shape has to do with being successful. You are not trying to make a team and it has nothing to do with playing sports. I've been in pretty good shape all my life from my basketball playing days. To this day I'm still working out and in good shape. Some may ask why would I continue to workout if I'm not playing basketball anymore. The answer is simple, as you get in better shape you will find that everything you do becomes easier. Walking up a flight of stairs is not as hard as it use to be and playing with your children or grandchildren doesn't wear you out. My job is very physically demanding. Being in good condition has help me overcome the physical demands and allows me to be more efficient. Being in shape can help extend your life. It is more than personal or physical appearance. The Harvard School of Public Health states, "When your heart and respiratory systems work well, you are at lower risk of developing heart disease or having a stroke." The Centers for Disease Control recommend at least 150 minutes of moderate-intense activity weekly to reap health benefits. The more you do the greater the results. When you are striving to unlock the doors to success in your life, it's going to be hard work. This is why your conditioning and being in shape is so vital. Throughout the course of the busy day you have many things going on and you have to have the energy to get things done with the least amount of effort. Good health allows you the energy to spend time with your family after work or school.

Hopefully you now understand the importance of exercising and staying in shape as part of your daily routine. Don't be the one to make excuses that you don't have the time. You have to make time. We make time to go to the hair dresser, go to the mall and the sports bar, as well as many other activities, but we don't make the time to be healthy and live longer productive lives.

I'm grateful that I have a workout routine that I consistently do. I have a demanding schedule that requires a lot of my time, not to mention my job consist of 12 hour shifts. Being in shape has allowed me to maintain a busy schedule without being tired at the end of the day. Make a decision today to look and feel better than ever. It's never to late to start and get in shape.

Chapter Six

Change Your Thinking

To achieve the things you want in life you have to change the way you have been thinking. If you continue to do the same things, you will continue to get the same results. We have to program our minds to do things differently if we find what we are doing isn't working. Our thinking has to be positive, no matter what has happened in the past. So what are you thinking about? The Bible states in Proverbs 23:7 that "As a man thinketh in his heart, so he becomes". You will become what you think about most. What you think about you bring about. The Bible states in Matthew 12:34 that "Out of the abundance of the heart the mouth speaks". In other words if you are thinking it you are going to speak it. Once you speak it you can't take it back and you will get just what you said. If you speak negatively, then negative things will be brought to fruition. This is called the "Law of Attraction".

The book, "The Secret" by Rhonda Byrne, talks about "Law of Attraction". My understanding is like attracts like. When you think about something over and over whether it is done conscientiously or not that is what enters your life. As I think about events in my life, I realize they were direct correlations to the thoughts I possessed. It doesn't matter who you are or where you are, the law of attraction is forming your entire life experience and it is being done through your thoughts. You become and attract what you think about most.

An example in my life occurred early in my marriage. My wife and I had been married about two years, with one vehicle and in need of a second car. At the time, we couldn't really afford it, so I began to say "someone is going to give me a car". My wife thought it was a far fetched idea but I really believed it would happen. I didn't know anything about the Law of Attraction. Within a few months, we were blessed with a car and clear title. Since then, I only think about the things I want to attract in my life.

Thoughts are magnetic and have a frequency. As you think them, they are sent out into the Universe and they magnetically attract all like things that are on the same frequency. Everything sent out returns to the source and that source is you.

Listening

What are you listening to each day? Whatever it maybe know that it will influence your day. I often hear people who are having a bad day say they got up on the wrong side of the bed. Well you don't have to get up on the wrong side. You have a choice about the side you get up on. When getting out of bed, the first thing we should do is listen to something positive or motivational to get us off to a great start. I have found in my personal life that listening to something positive or reading something positive influences a great day.

When riding in my car, I try to listen to something that's uplifting and positive. Stay away from all the negative things and be careful what you read in the newspaper. Don't focus on all the negativity going on in the world. It will only bring you down and affect your productivity throughout the day.

Reading

As I was matriculating through high school and college, there was nothing I disliked more than reading. I only did it when it was required. It was hard for me to open a book and read for leisure. It wasn't until I got married, that I began to develop a habit for reading. I noticed that every free moment my wife had, she was reading. I have never seen anyone read as much as she does and I couldn't understand her need to do it constantly. Then I noticed she had a very broad vocabulary, anytime I needed to know the definition of a word she knew it. If she didn't know the meaning she would quickly look it up and I'd hear it in her conversation soon after. She has one of the largest book collections I've ever seen. We have literally run out of space to put all her books. Thank goodness for e-readers, which she has two of.

Now she downloads all her books. As I began to read more, my vocabulary expanded and I was learning more than I ever had before. The more I learned the more I wanted to read. My goal is to read at least one book per month. I always reach that goal and sometimes more. Reading has change my life to the point that I'm writing this book. If it can change me, I'm confident it will change you as well. I saw a quote that stated "A man who does not read is no better then a man who can't read" and that is so true. I read where the average American only reads one book per year and the average self-made millionaire is reading one book per month.

We want our students to understand how important it is to not only read but understand what they are reading. It has been determine that many of our students are scoring low on their standardize tests because they can't read or fail to comprehend what they are reading. Until the children in the state of South Carolina learn to be proficient readers we will remain one of the lowest states when it comes to graduation. Readers become leaders.

Motivational speaker Zig Ziglar stated that information is exploding so fast that anyone who does not read and keep up is rapidly falling behind. If the person who reads 220 words per minute, will read for 20 minutes per day will read a total of 22 books of 100 pages each year.

I have a few "Quotes" I would like to share with you.

These are quotes that I use on a daily basis to help me get through the day or any other situation that my come up. I hope you enjoy them and are able to use some of them as needed:

"The problems that exist in the world today cannot be solved by the level of thinking that created them."
Albert Einstein

"Control your own destiny or someone else will."
Jack Welch

"There is a price for everything. Goodness is free, but greatness will cost you."
Delatorro McNeal

"Success is not about the destination: It's about the journey."
Unknown

"Information without application will lead to frustration."
Unknown

"If you commit yourself to making a difference, making a dollar in not hard."
Delatorra McNeal

"Doing what you like is freedom, liking what you do is happiness."
Johnny Carson

"Be the change that you want to see in the world."
Mahatma Gandhi

"Genius is one percent inspiration and ninety – nine percent perspiration."
Thomas Edison

"When you change the way you look at things, the things you look at change."
Wayne Dyer

"The tragedy of life is not that it ends so soon, but that we wait so long to begin it."
W. M. Lewis

"If life knocks you down, that's not your fault. But if I come back a week later, and you are still on the ground.........That's your fault."
Al Sharpton

"Good, better, best, never let it rest till your good is better and your better is best."
Unknown

"If you don't think every day is a good day, just try missing one."
Cavett Robert

"The only disability in life is a bad attitude."
Scott Hamilton

"When you set yourself on fire, the world will come to see you burn."
Dr. Dennis Kimbro

"We don't stop playing because we grow old; We grow old because we stop playing."
George Bernard Shaw

"Stop asking your time where it went, and start telling your time where to go."
Scott Thomas

"The only difference between the ordinary and the extraordinary is a little extra."
Unknown

"The core problem is not that we are too passionate about bad things, but that we are not passionate enough about good things."
Larry Crabb

"You are not what you think you are. What you think you are."
Unknown

Watch your thoughts; They become words
Watch your words; They become actions
Watch your actions; They become habits
Watch your habits; They become character
Watch your character; For it becomes your destiny!

Unknown

"Positive people don't react to life; they respond to it."
Unknown

"Plan ahead – it wasn't raining when Noah built the ark."
Richard Cushing

"You don't have to be great to start, But you have to start to be great."
Zig Ziglar

"Your career is what you are paid for; your calling is what you are made for."
Zig Ziglar

"You can make more friends in two months by becoming more interested in other people than you can in two years by trying to get people interested in you."
Dale Carnegle

"You can have everything in life you want if you will just help enough people get what they want."
Zig Ziglar

"We make a living by what we get; we make a life by what we give."
Winston Churchill

"It's better to be prepared for an opportunity and not have one than to have an opportunity and not be prepared."
Unknown

Dedication

To my wife of twenty-five years, Cheryl, I would like to thank you for allowing me the space and time to do the things I am passionate about. You have stood by me as I have coached and mentored young boys for 20 plus years, for this, I am grateful. You were there anytime I needed support, encouragement, or just a listening ear. You are one of the reasons I am writing this book and have become the person I am today. You have been the greatest mother to our children. Thank you and I love you.

Thanks to my children, who have allowed me to be the father I have always wanted to be. Crystal, Jay, Josh, and LaTera you have been the driving force and inspiration of the things I have done. You all have truly been a blessing in my life and I love you dearly.

I am grateful to God who has allowed me so many great opportunities.

Harvin L. Council, Sr.

About The Author

Harvin Council Sr. was born in Camden, S.C. He is a 1984 graduate of Jacksonville University. He has been married to Cheryl 25 years and they have three children.

I would love to hear from the readers of this book. Your feedback would be greatly appreciated. You can contact me at harvin.council@yahoo.com. Thank you for reading this book.

This is the 6 x 9 Basic Template. Paste your manuscript into this template or simply start typing. Delete this text prior to use.

www.ingramcontent.com/pod-product-compliance
Lightning Source LLC
Chambersburg PA
CBHW072035060426
42449CB00010BA/2274